AF596327

The Sangam's Embrace and beyond

Personal Journeys of Faith and Transformations

dradityamani@gmail.com

This book is a work of nonfiction.

ISBN:9798230859253

UBL:

https://books2read.com/u/bo5gw9

The stories are based on real events and people; any resemblance to other individuals or situations is purely coincidental.

Preface

This collection, The Sangam's Embrace and beyond, is a quiet celebration of the ordinary. It's a gathering of moments, observed and felt, woven together to create a tapestry of everyday life. These stories aren't about grand adventures or extraordinary feats, but rather the subtle nuances, the fleeting connections, and the quiet epiphanies that often go unnoticed in the rush of our daily routines. They are whispers from the heart of the mundane, offering glimpses into the beauty and complexity hidden within the seemingly simple. From the bustling energy of a local market to the quiet contemplation of a solitary walk, each piece in this collection attempts to capture the essence of a particular moment, a specific feeling. Some stories are born from personal experiences, reflections on encounters and observations that have lingered in my mind. Others are inspired by the world around me, the snippets of conversations overheard, the fleeting expressions on faces in a crowd, the vibrant tapestry of human interaction that unfolds before us every day.

Included in this collection is a narrative centered around the profound experience of the Prayagraj Kumbh Mela. This journey, a confluence of faith, humanity, and ancient tradition, left an indelible mark. I've attempted to capture the sheer scale and energy of this spiritual gathering, the vibrant colours, the resonant chants, and the palpable sense of devotion that permeated the air. It's a story not just of the event itself, but of the personal journey it inspired, a reflection on the search for meaning and the power of collective belief. These stories are, in essence, invitations. Invitations to pause, to observe, to reflect. Invitations to see the extraordinary in the ordinary, the profound in the commonplace. I hope that within these pages, you'll find echoes of

your own experiences, moments that resonate with your own understanding of the world. More than anything, I hope these stories offer a gentle reminder that even in the midst of the everyday, there is always something to discover, something to cherish, something to celebrate. Enjoy the journey.

Introduction

Life, in its intricate tapestry of moments, weaves a story that is both uniquely personal and universally shared. It's in the quiet hum of a morning commute, the shared laughter over a meal, the fleeting connection with a stranger, that the true essence of our existence unfolds. This book, The Sangam's Embrace and beyond, is a collection of these everyday stories, glimpses into the lives of ordinary people navigating the extraordinary landscape of daily

life.
These narratives are born from observation, from listening to the whispers of the world around me, and from reflecting on the experiences that have shaped my own journey. They are not grand tales of adventure, but rather intimate portraits of humanity in its myriad forms – the joys, the sorrows, the triumphs, and the quiet moments of reflection that make up the fabric of our lives.
Within these pages, you'll encounter a diverse cast of

characters: the shopkeeper with

a hidden story, the young couple navigating the complexities of love, the elderly woman reminiscing about a life well-lived. Each story is a window into a different world, a different perspective, a different way of experiencing the human condition.

A significant part of this collection is dedicated to my journey to the Prayagraj Mahakumbh. This monumental gathering of faith and humanity was an experience that transcended the ordinary. The sheer scale of the event, the vibrant tapestry of cultures and beliefs, the palpable sense of devotion – all of these elements left an indelible mark. The narrative surrounding the Kumbh is not just a travelogue, but a personal reflection on faith, community, and the search for meaning in a world that often feels chaotic and overwhelming. It's an attempt to capture the spiritual resonance of this ancient ritual and its impact on the millions who gather to partake in its sacred waters.

This book is an invitation to slow down, to pay attention to the small details, to find the extraordinary within the ordinary. It's a celebration of the human spirit, its resilience, its vulnerability, and its capacity for connection. I hope that these stories resonate with you, sparking your own memories and reflections on the beauty and complexity of everyday life. Welcome to the journey.

Is it a Train? Is It a Plane? No, It's Just a Very Late Mukesh

The clock glared at us, its hands mocking our increasingly frantic dance. My wife, bless her organized soul, had meticulously planned our trip. Train tickets? Booked. Snacks? Packed. Outfits? Coordinated (a fact she reminded me of repeatedly). The only snag? Our driver, Mukesh, was running on "Indian Standard Time," which, as everyone knows, is a flexible concept bordering on abstract art.

"He said 'ten minutes' twenty minutes ago!" I exclaimed, pacing like a caged tiger. My wife, usually serene, was now channeling her inner drill sergeant. "Call him again! Tell him if we miss this train, he's walking back to his home"
I dialed Mukesh. “Mukesh, where are you? The train leaves in an hour! We're going to miss it!"
"Sir, traffic," he mumbled, a symphony of horns blaring in the background. "But don't worry, I'm nearby.
Another ten minutes ticked by,

each second an agonizing hammer blow to our travel plans. Finally, a beat-up activa appeared, driven by a harried-looking Mukesh. "Sorry, sir, madam," he panted. "There was a… a cow in the road. A very stubborn cow."
We piled into the car, my wife shooting Mukesh a look that could curdle milk. As we sped towards the station, Mukesh regaled us with tales of the stubborn cow, its extended family, and the ensuing traffic chaos. We arrived at the station

just as the train whistle blew. We sprinted, luggage flying, and leaped onto the train just as the doors closed. We collapsed into our seats, breathless, disheveled, and strangely, slightly amused. The moral of the story? When traveling in India, always factor in "cow time."

My Taste Buds Went on Vacation

The rhythmic clatter of the train wheels was a soothing soundtrack to my anticipation. I'd boarded, settled into my seat, and was ready for that quintessential Indian train journey experience: the chai. The chaiwala arrived, his call echoing down the aisle, a promise of warmth and sweet, milky goodness. I eagerly flagged him down and accepted a steaming paper cup.

Taking a sip, I braced myself for

the familiar explosion of flavor. Instead, my taste buds registered…
nothing. Absolutely nothing. It was like drinking slightly warm water that had vaguely heard of tea. I took another sip, trying to discern even a hint of tea. Nope. It was the culinary equivalent of a blank canvas.
I looked around. Other passengers were happily slurping their chai, their faces registering varying degrees of satisfaction. Were they all experiencing this flavorless

beverage and just politely pretending it was delicious? Was this some kind of mass delusion?

I discreetly flagged down the chaiwala again. "Bhaiya," I whispered, "this chai… it tastes like… water."

He looked at me, slightly offended. "Chai? Madam, this is special chai! Very… healthy chai!"

"Healthy how?" I asked. "Does it… hydrate extra well?"

He shrugged. "It has… less… everything. Less sugar, less

milk, less tea… very good for… digestion!"

Ah, digestion. Of course. My digestive system was clearly thrilled to be processing warm, vaguely tea-scented water.

I resigned myself to my fate. I took another sip of the watery chai, trying to imagine the robust flavor that should have been there. Maybe if I closed my eyes and concentrated really hard… nope. Still water.

From then on, every time the chaiwala passed, I politely declined, offering a weak smile. I even started carrying my own tea bags, just in case. The lesson

I learned? On Indian trains, sometimes the chai is an adventure. Sometimes, it's just... water. But hey, at least it's hydrating.

The Sacred Dip

The biting winter wind nipped at my exposed skin as I set off before dawn. Prayagraj, and the holy Sangam, was my destination. Thirty kilometers lay ahead, a pilgrimage I'd undertaken on foot. The pull of the sacred confluence of the Ganga, Yamuna, and Saraswati rivers was stronger than the discomfort in my aching muscles.

The sun rose, painting the sky in hues of orange and pink, but the chill remained. Small villages

dotted the landscape, offering glimpses into rural life. The aroma of woodsmoke and cow dung hung in the air. As I walked, I chanted prayers, the rhythm of my steps matching the rhythm of the mantras.

By mid-morning, the crowds began to thicken. Pilgrims, like me, were converging on the Sangam from all directions. The road transformed into a sea of humanity, a vibrant tapestry of colors and languages. The air buzzed with chants, devotional songs, and the excited chatter of

families.
The last few kilometers were the toughest. The sun beat down mercilessly, and my throat was parched. The tantalizing smell of hot tea and pakoras wafted from roadside stalls, a welcome distraction. I stopped for a quick refuel, the warmth of the tea spreading through my chilled bones. The crispy pakoras, spiced just right, were a taste of heaven.
Finally, the Sangam came into view. The sight was breathtaking. The vast expanse

of the rivers, the confluence marked by the distinct colors of the Ganga and Yamuna, and the throngs of devotees taking holy dips – it was a spectacle of faith. The traffic jam near the bathing ghats was a chaotic ballet of vehicles and people. But none of that mattered. I had reached my destination. I joined the throng, the cold water of the Sangam washing away my fatigue and filling me with a sense of peace. The 30-kilometer walk had been

arduous, but the spiritual
reward was immeasurable.

The Battle for the Bus's Best Seat

The bus lurched, groaning like a dyspeptic elephant, as we embarked on our pilgrimage to the Sangam. Thirty-odd ladies, armed with thermoses of chai and enough snacks to feed a small army, filled the bus with a cacophony of chatter. But the bonhomie quickly evaporated as we hit the first series of potholes.

Suddenly, Mrs. Chaturvedi, known for her delicate constitution, clutched her stomach. "Oh dear," she moaned,

"I think I need some fresh air." Before anyone could react, she'd lurched towards the front of the bus, the universal sign for impending nausea. The driver, a seasoned veteran of such pilgrimages, sighed and pointed to the designated "vomit zone" – the very front entrance of the bus.
Within minutes, the front of the bus became prime real estate. Mrs. Sharma, who'd been regaling everyone with tales of her prize-winning

petunias, suddenly turned a peculiar shade

of green and elbowed Mrs. Chaturvedi aside. “Excuse me,” she gasped, “priority seating!”

The competition was fierce. Auntie Meena, who'd been happily knitting a particularly hideous orange sweater, now clutched it like a life raft, her eyes fixed on the horizon (or rather, the rapidly approaching trees). “I always get car sick,” she declared, her voice a little too loud, hoping to assert her claim.

The driver, meanwhile, was trying to navigate the chaotic road while simultaneously dispensing paper bags like a harried croupier. “Ladies, ladies,” he yelled over the din, “there’s enough space for everyone to… uh… express themselves!”

The scene at the front of the bus resembled a chaotic audition for a dramatic society play, with each lady vying for the coveted "vomit zone" spot. Mrs. Joshi, armed with a packet of ginger biscuits (a supposed cure-all), tried to maintain a semblance of dignity while simultaneously trying to secure her place in the queue.

Finally, after what seemed like an eternity, we reached the Sangam. The ladies, a little greener around the gills but otherwise intact, disembarked, ready for their holy dip. The front of the bus, however, bore the unmistakable signs of the journey – a testament to the power of bad roads and the collective anxiety of thirty women on a pilgrimage.

Scooty, Sangam, and Shenanigans

The lure of the Sangam's holy waters was irresistible, but our budget was tighter than a drum. A rickshaw was out of the question, and a taxi? Forget about it. Then, we spotted it: a lone, slightly battered scooty, parked invitingly by the roadside. "Tripling?" my friend Rohan suggested, a mischievous glint in his eye. "Sangam here we come!" I hesitated. Tripling was definitely against the rules, and this scooty looked like it might fall apart if we sneezed too hard. But the pull of the Ganga was strong. We haggled with the owner, a wiry man with a handlebar mustache, and soon, we were off, three adults perched precariously on the tiny vehicle.

Rohan, the self-proclaimed expert driver, took the lead, with me sandwiched in the middle and our other friend, Priya, clinging to the back like a limpet. The scooty sputtered and coughed, protesting loudly against our combined weight. We wobbled through the crowded streets, dodging stray dogs, errant cyclists, and the occasional cow. Every bump sent us flying, and I swear I saw Priya's life flash before her eyes at least twice. The journey was a comedy of errors. At one point, Rohan nearly drove us into a pile of coconuts. Another time, Priya's dupatta got caught in the wheel, bringing us to a screeching halt. But through it all, we laughed, the sheer absurdity of our situation making the journey an adventure in itself.

Finally, we reached the Sangam. We parked the scooty haphazardly and joined the throngs of devotees rushing towards the holy waters. The dip was everything we'd hoped for – a moment of peace and spiritual cleansing.

After our refreshing dip, we returned to find the scooty exactly where we'd left it. The owner, surprisingly, was nowhere to be seen. We hopped on, ready

for the return journey. But just as we started the engine, the owner reappeared, waving frantically. He pointed towards a distant parking lot. "Parking," he yelled, "far away!"

It turned out the spot where we'd parked was a no-parking zone. Our "expert" driver, Rohan, had unwittingly parked us in the worst possible place. With a sigh, the owner took over, and we followed him on foot for what seemed like miles. We finally reached the designated parking spot, hot, tired, and slightly embarrassed. But as we looked back at the Sangam, shimmering in the distance, we couldn't help but smile. Our tripling adventure, though chaotic, had gotten us there. And that's all that mattered.

Flavors of Faith

The crisp morning air nipped at our noses as we navigated the bustling Prayagraj market, a vibrant prelude to our Sangam dip. The aroma of spices and frying oil hung heavy in the air, a tantalizing invitation to indulge. Our stomachs rumbled in agreement.

First stop: a steaming cauldron of milk, its surface topped with a thick layer of creamy froth. The vendor ladled out generous mugs, the warmth spreading through our chilled hands. We sipped slowly, savoring the rich, sweet flavor, a perfect start to our culinary adventure. Next, the irresistible scent of pakoras drew us in. A mountain of golden-brown fritters, glistening with oil and sprinkled with chaat masala, sat piled high. We ordered a plateful, the crispy exterior giving way to a soft, spiced potato and vegetable filling. Each bite was an explosion of flavor, the perfect accompaniment to the hot milk.

Our market stroll continued, and

soon, we stumbled upon a tiny stall overflowing with freshly baked buns. "Bun-butter," Rohan declared, his eyes lighting up. We grabbed a couple, the soft, buttery buns melting in our mouths. Simple, yet utterly delicious.

The final temptation was a samosa stall, the air thick with the aroma of fried pastry and spiced potatoes. We couldn't resist. The samosas were huge, triangular parcels of goodness, filled with a savory mixture of potatoes, peas, and spices. The crispy, flaky crust added another layer of texture, making each bite a delight.

We found a quiet corner amidst the market chaos and sat down to enjoy our feast. The hot milk warmed us from the inside out, while the pakoras, bun-butter, and samosas satisfied our hunger. The market buzzed around us, a symphony of sounds and smells, but we were lost in our own little world of culinary bliss.

As we finished the last samosa, a sense of contentment settled over us. Our market trip had been a delicious adventure, a perfect way to fuel up for our Sangam dip. With our stomachs full and our spirits high, we continued our journey, the promise of the holy waters now even more enticing. The flavors of the market, the hot milk, the crispy pakoras, the buttery buns, and the spicy samosas, would linger in our memories long after the Sangam dip.

Dubey Ji's Holy Tobacco and Honest Guidance

Our Prayagraj guide, a portly fellow named Dubey ji, had a permanent bulge in his cheek. It wasn't a tumor, but a generous wad of tobacco. He spoke around it, his words sometimes muffled, sometimes punctuated by a sudden, vigorous cheek-rubbing maneuver. Despite this, Dubey ji was a gem. "Welcome, welcome," he mumbled, the tobacco bulge shifting precariously. "I will show you the real Prayagraj." And he did. He was brutally honest. "That temple? Tourist trap. Avoid." He pointed to another, smaller temple. "This one? Actually quite nice. And less crowded."

Dubey ji was also surprisingly caring. He fussed over us like a mother hen, making sure we had enough water, reminding us to wear sunscreen, and even negotiating discounts at the local shops. "Bargaining is an art," he'd say, winking, the tobacco bulge wobbling.

His driving was… well, let's just say he had a unique style. He navigated the chaotic Prayagraj traffic with a combination of bravado and prayer, honking his horn incessantly and somehow managing to avoid collisions by what seemed like sheer luck. "These drivers," he'd mutter, shaking his head, "they have no respect for the road… or for my tobacco."

But the best thing about Dubey ji was his knowledge of the Sangam. He didn't just take us to the main ghat, where the crowds

were thick and the water murky. He took us to a quieter spot, a little further downstream, where the confluence of the rivers was clearer and the atmosphere more serene. "This," he declared, spitting a stream of brown juice into a discreetly placed container, "this is the real Sangam. The holy dip should be peaceful, not a wrestling match."

He even helped us perform the rituals, explaining the significance of each step. "Now, dip three times,"

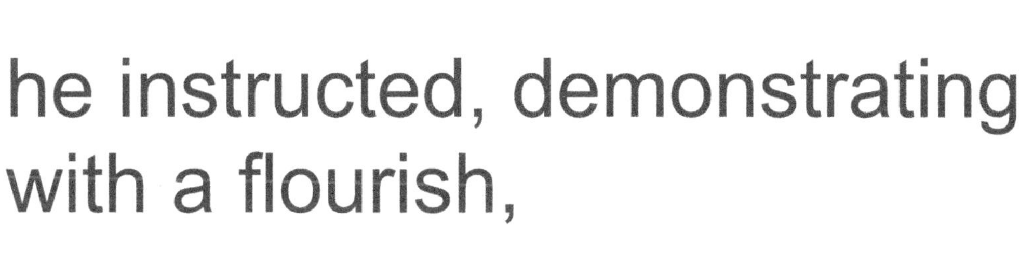

he instructed, demonstrating with a flourish,

"and pray for… well, pray for whatever you want. Just be sincere."
After the dip, as we were drying ourselves, Dubey ji offered us each a piece of candy. "A little something sweet after the purification," he said, beaming. The tobacco bulge seemed to have shrunk slightly. Maybe it was the holy water. Or maybe it was just Dubey ji's good nature shining through. Either way, we were grateful for his guidance, his honesty, his caring nature, and even his… unique driving

style. He was, after all, the best tobacco-chewing, honest, caring, good-driving, Sangam-savvy guide we could have asked for.

Traffic to Nirvana

Our Kumbh Mela 2025 pilgrimage started with the best of intentions. We envisioned serene dips in the Sangam, soul-stirring chants, and a general sense of spiritual upliftment. What we got was a day-long wrestling match with Prayagraj's legendary traffic. We left our hotel at the crack of dawn, armed with thermos flasks of chai and enough snacks to survive a small apocalypse. "Early bird gets the worm,"

Rohan declared, confidently navigating our rented minivan. Famous last words. Barely had we cleared the city limits when we hit the first snag. A herd of cows, seemingly engaged in a philosophical debate, had decided to stage a sit-in right in the middle of the road. An hour later, we were still moo-ving at a snail's pace.
The traffic jam was a beast of its own. It wasn't just cars; it was a chaotic ballet of buses, trucks, rickshaws, scooters,

and pilgrims on foot, all vying for the same

patch of road. Horns blared incessantly, creating a symphony of urban frustration. Our minivan became a mobile picnic spot as we polished off our chai and started on the snacks.

As the sun climbed higher, so did our tempers. Rohan, usually the epitome of calm, started muttering darkly about the "karmic consequences" of traffic jams. Priya, who had brought a book on meditation to enhance our spiritual experience, was now using it to swat away flies.

Lunchtime arrived, and we were

still miles from the Sangam. We ordered food from a roadside dhaba, the delivery boy navigating the traffic jam on a motorbike with the agility of a circus performer. We ate our lukewarm dal and roti in the minivan, watching the world go by at approximately 2 kilometers per hour.

The entire day was a blur of honking, waiting, and existential questioning. We saw the same auto-rickshaw driver three times, and each time, he gave us a knowing nod, as if to say, "We're

all in this together."
Finally, as the sun began to set, we limped towards the Sangam. The holy dip, initially the highlight of our trip, now seemed like a distant dream. We managed a quick, rushed dip, the cold water a welcome relief from the sweltering minivan.
By the time we got back to our hotel, it was late. We were exhausted, frustrated, and slightly delirious. "Well," Rohan said, collapsing onto his bed, "at least we had a

memorable Kumbh Mela." Memorable

indeed. We may not have found spiritual enlightenment, but we certainly achieved a new level of patience. And we learned a valuable lesson: next time, we're walking.

Dressed for Divinity

February 7th, 2025. The air in Prayagraj crackled with anticipation for the Sangam dip. We, however, were experiencing a different kind of crackle – the sound of our carefully laid plans disintegrating. We'd envisioned a serene, spiritual experience, a cleansing of the soul. What we got was a frantic scramble for… well, clothes.

See, we'd packed everything: towels, toiletries, even those little plastic bags for wet clothes. What we'd forgotten? The actual clothes to wear for the dip. They were all neatly folded in the trunk of our car, parked a mile away. "Don't panic," Rohan said, trying to project an air of calm that he clearly didn't feel. "We'll just buy some new clothes." Easy for him to say. He wasn't the one who'd have to explain to his wife why he'd bought a pair of bright orange "Hare Krishna" pants. The market near the Sangam was a kaleidoscope of colors and chaos. Vendors hawked their

wares, pilgrims jostled for space, and the air buzzed with a thousand different conversations. We plunged into the throng, like salmon swimming upstream.

Finding suitable attire for a holy dip proved to be more challenging than we'd anticipated. Priya wanted something "respectful but not too flashy." I just wanted something that wouldn't disintegrate the moment it touched water. Rohan, meanwhile, was eyeing a stall selling t-shirts with pictures of various deities, clearly intending to make a fashion statement.

After much haggling and frantic searching, we emerged, victorious, but slightly traumatized. Priya had found a simple kurta-pajama set. I'd opted for a slightly less garish version of Rohan's "Hare Krishna" pants (a muted yellow, thank you very much). And Rohan? He was now the proud owner of a t-shirt featuring a particularly flamboyant depiction of Lord Shiva.

We finally made it to the Sangam, a little later than planned, and a little poorer. As we stood on the banks of the holy river, dressed in our hastily acquired attire, we couldn't help but laugh. Our spiritual journey had taken an unexpected detour, but it had certainly been memorable. And hey, at least we had a funny story to tell. Plus, Rohan's Shiva t-shirt was a guaranteed conversation starter.

When the Journey is the Destination

Our 2025 Prayagraj Kumbh Mela adventure began with a single, noble goal: to experience the divine confluence of the Ganga, Yamuna, and Saraswati rivers. We'd booked tents well in advance, envisioning cozy evenings after our holy dips. What we hadn't envisioned was the sheer, glorious chaos of the Mela. We arrived, bright-eyed and bushy-tailed, ready to embrace the spiritual experience. Our tent booking confirmation was clutched firmly in Rohan's hand, our beacon of hope in the sea of humanity. The directions, however, were vague. "Sector 4, near the… uh… big tree." There were approximately a million big trees.

We wandered, like lost souls, through the tent city, a labyrinth of canvas and bamboo. Every tent looked the same. Every path seemed to lead back to where we started. We asked for directions, but everyone was

either equally lost or too busy chanting to pay attention. One helpful soul pointed us towards a “Sector 4” that, after a two-hour trek, turned out to be a completely different Sector 4. As the sun began to set, casting long shadows across the tent city, our spirits began to flag. We were hot, tired, and starting to resemble pilgrims who’d been on a slightly too-long pilgrimage. “Maybe,” Priya suggested, “we should just… give up?”

Just then, as if by divine intervention (or perhaps just

dumb luck), we crested a small rise and saw them. Our tents. In the distance. Across a vast, unnavigable expanse of tents, people, and the occasional sacred cow. They were so close, yet so far. Like an oasis mirage in the desert of canvas.

"Well," Rohan said, a wry smile spreading across his face, "at least we know they exist."

We decided to cut our losses. The Sangam beckoned, and we were in desperate need of a cleansing dip. We trudged towards the holy waters, leaving

our distant tents to their lonely fate.

The dip was glorious. The cool water washed away the frustration of the day, and as we stood on the banks, watching the sun set over the Mela, we could just make out our tents in the distance, tiny specks of canvas against the vast backdrop.

“Look,” I said, pointing towards them. “Our tents! They’re waving at us!”

Rohan chuckled. “They’re probably just as relieved as we are that we’re not coming back tonight."

We might not have reached our booked tents, but we had reached the Sangam. And in the end, that's what mattered. Besides, we now had a great story to tell – a story about faith, perseverance, and the elusive nature of tent cities.

The Unsung Hero of the Indian Railways

The train lurched and swayed, a rhythmic dance of steel on steel. Most passengers were engrossed in their phones, oblivious to the world outside the window. But I watched, fascinated, as a lone figure moved through the carriage, a whirlwind of efficiency. He wasn't just cleaning; he was dedicating himself to it.

His name, I later learned, was Prakash. He wasn't just wiping down seats; he was scrubbing them, attacking grime with the fervor of a seasoned warrior. He wasn't just sweeping; he was meticulously clearing every nook and cranny, chasing dust bunnies into oblivion. His brow was beaded with sweat, his movements tireless. He worked with a quiet intensity, a sense of pride in his craft.

I watched as he tackled a particularly stubborn stain on the floor. He didn't just dab at it; he knelt, scrubbed, and then inspected his work with a critical

eye. Satisfied, he moved on, leaving behind a spotless patch in his wake. It wasn't just a job for Prakash; it was a mission.

He moved through the carriage, his presence a silent testament to hard work and dedication. He didn't complain, he didn't slack off, he simply cleaned. He treated the train, this rolling metal beast, with a respect that many of its passengers didn't. He was a guardian of cleanliness, a silent hero of the rails.

As he passed my seat, I couldn't help but smile. "You're doing a

fantastic job," I said.
He paused, a flicker of surprise on his face. Then, a wide, genuine smile spread across his features. "Thank you, sir," he said, his voice warm. "It's my duty."
Prakash's dedication was a small but powerful reminder that even the most mundane tasks can be imbued with purpose and pride. He wasn't just cleaning a train; he was creating a more pleasant journey for everyone on board. He was a reminder that dignity and dedication can be found in

any profession, and that even the smallest acts of service can make a big difference. As the train pulled into the station, I watched Prakash move on to the next carriage, his broom and dustpan his weapons in the ongoing battle against grime. He was a true inspiration.

Market Modern

The familiar cacophony of the Tuesday vegetable market had taken on a decidedly modern hum. Old Man Ghanshyam, his weathered face usually creased in a frown as he haggled, now sported a pair of spectacles perched on his nose, scanning a QR code on a customer's phone. His ancient brass scales, which had witnessed decades of vegetable weigh-ins, were replaced by a sleek electronic version that flashed digital numbers with each plop of a tomato.

Even the lighting had undergone a transformation. The dim kerosene lamps, which once cast dancing shadows across the mounds of produce, were gone. Bright LED lights, strung overhead like a festive garland, illuminated every vibrant shade of green, red, and purple. The market, once a stage for theatrical bargaining under the flickering light, felt almost clinical in its brightness.

Young Rani, Ghanshyam's

granddaughter, was the driving force behind these changes. She'd convinced him that adopting these new technologies would not only make his life easier but also attract more customers. Initially resistant, Ghanshyam now admitted, grudgingly, that she had been right. The QR code payments were faster, no more fumbling with damp notes and loose change. The electronic scale was precise, eliminating any disputes about weight. And the LED lights, well, they just made

everything look so much better. The shift wasn't without its quirks. Ghanshyam still occasionally patted his pockets instinctively, reaching for imaginary coins. He sometimes struggled to explain the digital transactions to his older, less tech-savvy customers. But even they were adapting, drawn in by the convenience and the brighter, more welcoming atmosphere. The Tuesday market, a cornerstone of tradition, had embraced modernity, proving that even the most rooted customs could evolve with the times. The aroma of fresh vegetables still hung in the air, but now it mingled with the quiet whir of progress.

Banana Peel Blues

Principal Pradeep was a man of great intellect and even greater stubbornness. He ran his school like a tight ship, believing in discipline and order above all else. So, when he slipped on a stray banana peel in the staffroom and heard a sickening crack, he refused to acknowledge the obvious: he'd broken his leg.

"It's just a sprain," he declared, hopping around on one foot. "A bit of rest and I'll be right as rain."

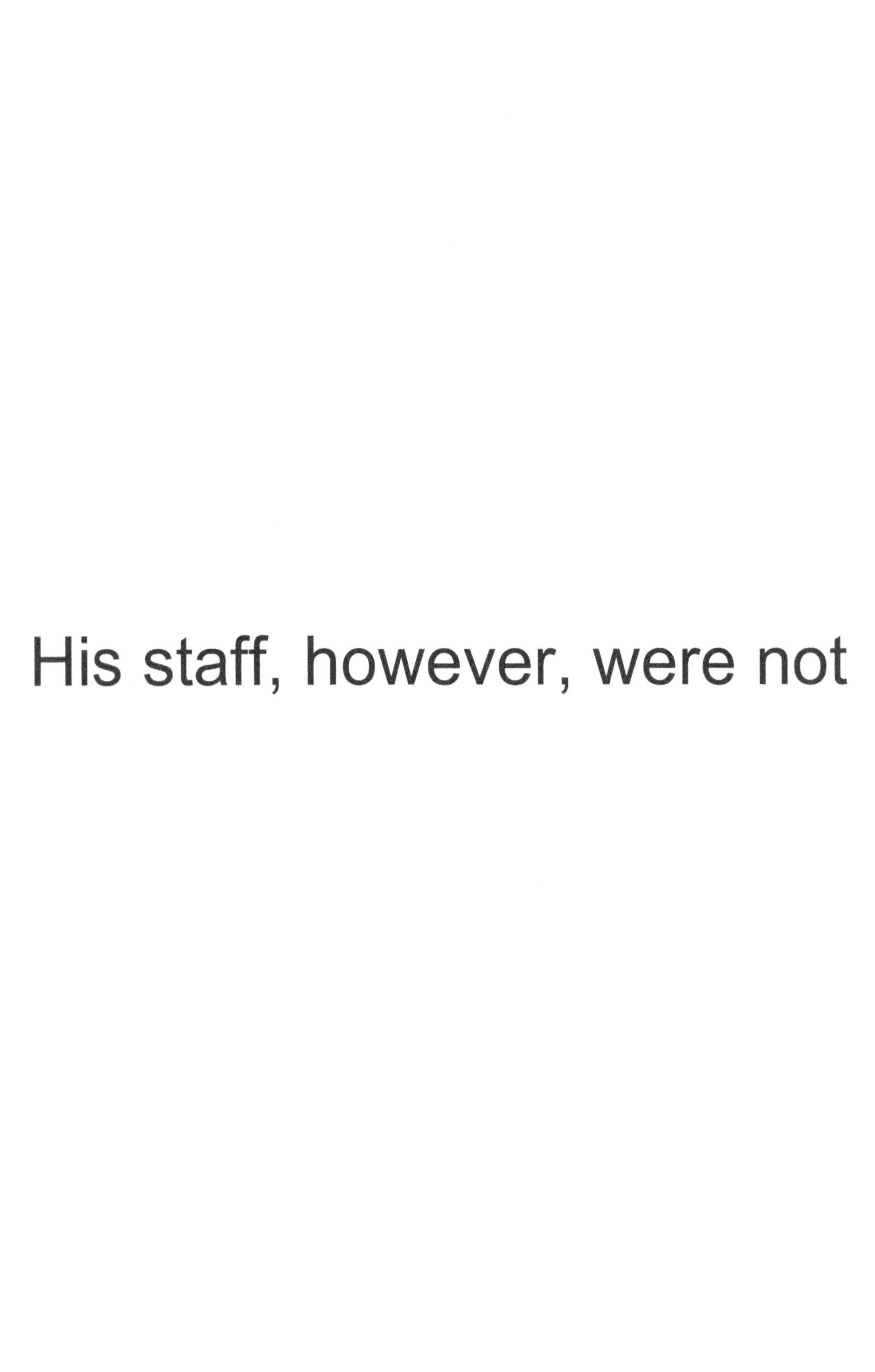
His staff, however, were not

convinced. They watched in amusement and concern as Principal Pradeep attempted to conduct assembly while balancing precariously on a stool, his leg swollen and turning an alarming shade of purple.
"Sir," his deputy principal, Mrs. Sharma, pleaded, "please, let us take you to the hospital."
"Nonsense!" he retorted, waving his hand dismissively. "I have a school to run!"
And so, Principal Pradeep continued his daily routine, hobbling through the corridors,

conducting classes while propping his leg up on a chair, and even attempting to climb the stairs to his office (a feat that ended with him sliding back down on his bottom). The students, of course, found the whole situation hilarious. They started a betting pool on how long it would take for him to admit defeat, and some even took to imitating his hopping gait, much to the amusement of their parents. Finally, after a week of this charade, Principal Pradeep's leg had swollen to twice its normal size, and the pain had become so excruciating that he could barely move. Even he had to admit that maybe, just maybe, he needed a doctor.

At the hospital, the doctor took one look at his leg and burst out laughing. "What on earth have you been doing?" he asked, shaking his head in disbelief.

Principal Pradeep mumbled something about a banana peel and a slight miscalculation. The doctor just

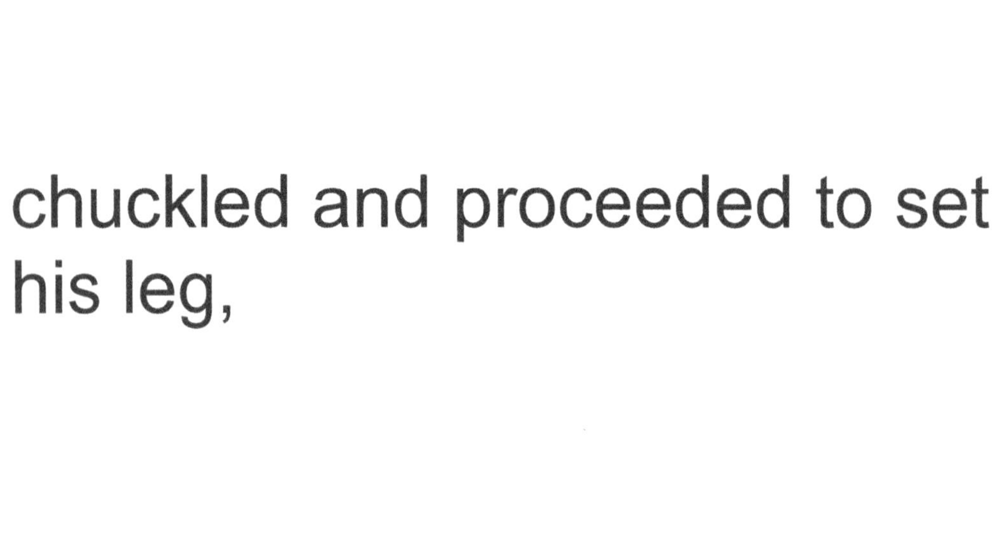
chuckled and proceeded to set his leg,

informing him that he would need a cast and crutches for the next six weeks.

As Principal Pradeep hobbled out of the hospital, he couldn't help but smile. He might have been stubborn, but he was also a good sport. And besides, he knew that his students would have a field day with this story, and that was worth a broken leg any day.

Dust Devils and Determination

The "BreathEasy" organization was born from a collective cough. Residents of the dusty town of Dhulnagar were choking. Trucks laden with dry sand, essential for construction, roared through their streets, leaving behind clouds of particulate matter. Children developed respiratory problems, the elderly were housebound, and even the hardiest residents felt the sting in their eyes and lungs. BreathEasy decided enough was

enough.
Their initial attempts were met with apathy. Construction companies, citing tight deadlines and cost concerns, dismissed their pleas. Local authorities, overwhelmed by other issues, offered sympathetic nods but little action. BreathEasy members, a mix of teachers, shopkeepers, and concerned parents, felt disheartened. They organized rallies, wrote letters to the editor, and even tried peaceful

protests, only to be met with dust and indifference.

But they refused to give up. They started small, documenting the truck movements with photos and videos, creating a stark visual record of the pollution. They organized free health check-ups, highlighting the link between the dust and respiratory illnesses. They engaged with the media, their stories of suffering and resilience slowly gaining traction.

Their breakthrough came when a local school principal, inspired by their efforts, involved his students. The children created

artwork depicting the dusty streets and wrote poignant letters to local officials. This caught the attention of a regional environmental group, who joined BreathEasy's cause, providing legal and technical expertise.

Finally, the authorities took notice. Stricter regulations were implemented, mandating covered trucks and designated routes. Construction companies, facing fines and public pressure, complied. The dust began to settle, literally and figuratively.

BreathEasy's victory wasn't just about cleaner air; it was a testament to the power of collective action. They had transformed apathy into empathy, indifference into action. Dhulnagar could finally breathe easy, thanks to a group of determined citizens who refused to be silenced by the dust.

Beyond the Badge

Constable Durga Bai's uniform was crisp, her demeanor unwavering, but her feet screamed in silent agony. At 59, with a hairline fracture in her right foot, every step was a battle. Twelve-hour shifts at the bustling city police station were a marathon of pain, but Durga Bai gritted her teeth and pushed through. Retirement was just around the corner, a beacon of hope in the relentless grind, but until then, duty called.

Her day began before sunrise. A quick, frugal breakfast, and she was out the door, the rhythmic throb in her foot a constant companion. The station hummed with activity – ringing phones, hurried reports, and the constant flow of people. Durga Bai, despite her limp, navigated the chaos with practiced ease. She registered complaints, mediated minor disputes, and offered a steady presence in the midst of the city's churn.

Lunch was a hurried affair, a few bites snatched between calls.

There was no time for a proper meal, no time for rest. Her foot throbbed louder with each passing hour, but she couldn't afford to slow down. The station was short-staffed, leaves were a luxury, and Durga Bai knew her colleagues were stretched thin as well. She was a pillar of support, her experience invaluable, even with her injury.

Evenings were the toughest. Fatigue gnawed at her, the pain in her foot intensified, but she kept going. She thought of her family, their faces etched in her

mind – her children, now grown, and her grandchildren, who filled her heart with joy. She longed to spend time with them, to play with them, to simply relax in their company. But duty came first. There was no time for physiotherapy, no time for proper medical attention. The small salary barely covered household expenses, and specialized treatment was a distant dream. She relied on pain relievers, popping them discreetly throughout the day, a temporary shield against the relentless ache.

Her colleagues admired her dedication. They saw the pain she endured, the unwavering commitment she displayed. They offered to help, to take on some of her workload, but Durga Bai refused. She didn't want to burden them further. She would bear her pain, she told them, until retirement finally arrived.

Her nights were short, sleep often interrupted by the throbbing in her foot. But as the first rays of dawn touched the

horizon, Durga Bai would rise again, her uniform starched, her spirit unbroken. She was a symbol of resilience, a testament to the strength of the human spirit. She was Durga Bai, the constable with the aching foot and the unwavering dedication, counting down the days until she could finally hang up her uniform and tend to her own needs, but until then, she would serve and protect, one painful step at a time. Her story was a quiet inspiration, a reminder that even in the face of adversity, duty and

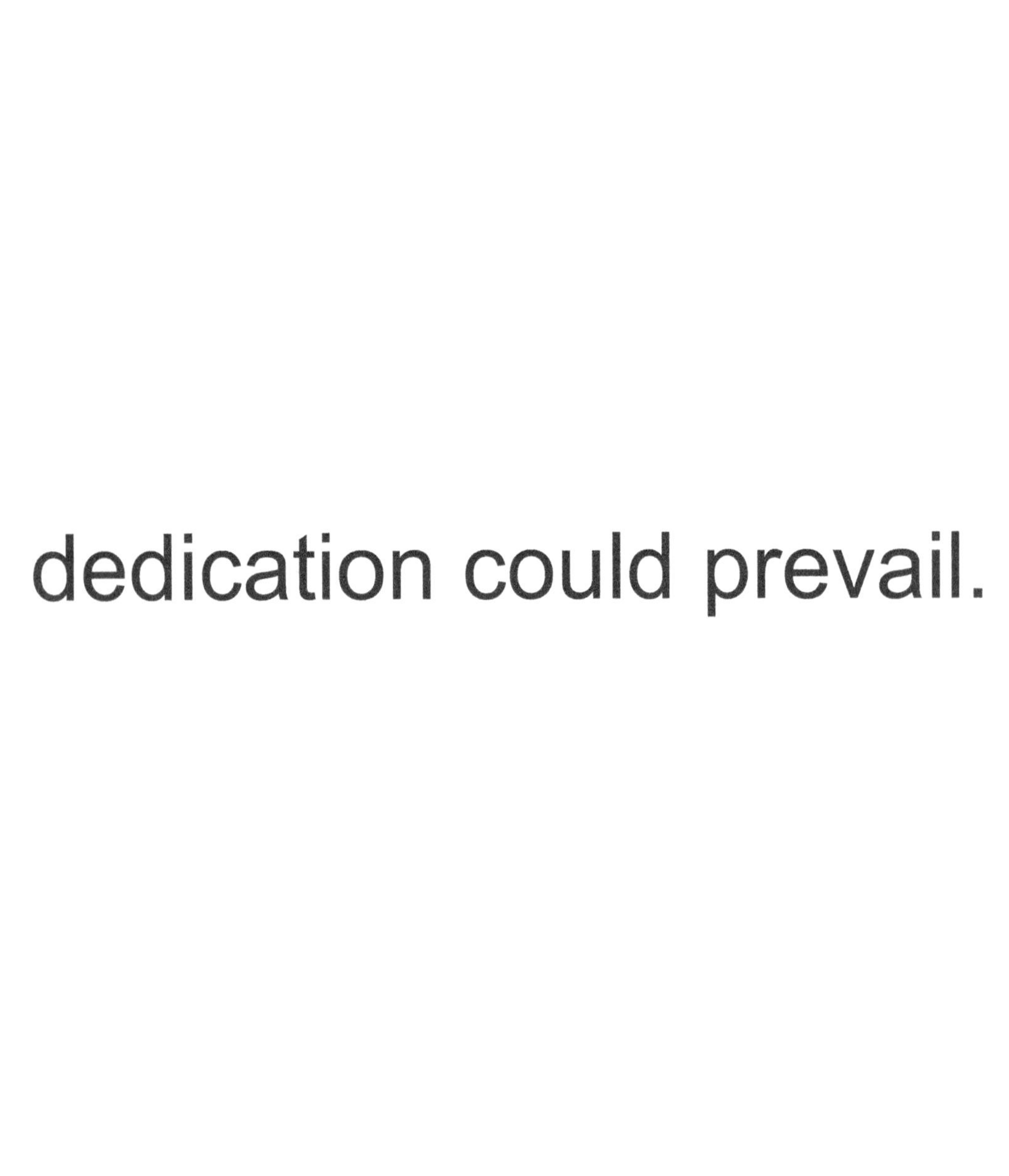

dedication could prevail.

A Legacy of Fire and Flour

In the heart of Guatemala, where ancient Mayan traditions intertwine with modern life, the art of tortilla making has become more than just a culinary practice—it's a vibrant symbol of cultural preservation. Women like Maria, Juana, and Esperanza, inheritors of this ancestral knowledge, honor their heritage by crafting these humble flatbreads, keeping alive the legacy of their ancestors.

The process begins with

"nixtamalization," an age-old technique where corn kernels are soaked in lime water, cooked, and then hulled. This transformative process not only enhances the nutritional value of the corn but also unlocks its unique flavor. The resulting "masa," or dough, is then meticulously ground using a traditional stone mill or "metate," a practice passed down through families for centuries. Luisa, with her strong hands and generations of wisdom guiding her, expertly grinds the masa,

her movements rhythmic and precise.
With skilled hands and a deep connection to their roots, these women shape the masa into perfect circles, each one a testament to their dedication and artistry. Elena, a young woman learning from her elders, carefully molds each tortilla, her fingers dancing across the dough with newfound confidence. The tortillas are then cooked on a hot griddle called a "comal," where they puff up and

develop those signature charred spots that

speak of tradition and authenticity. Sofia, her face glowing from the heat of the comal, flips each tortilla with practiced ease, ensuring they are cooked to perfection. These tortillas are more than just sustenance; they are a tangible link to the past, a culinary embodiment of Mayan resilience and ingenuity. They grace tables at every meal, accompanying vibrant stews, flavorful beans, and spicy salsas. Each bite is a reminder of the rich tapestry of

Guatemalan culture, woven with

threads of history, community, and ancestral wisdom.

In a world that often prioritizes convenience and speed, these indigenous communities stand as guardians of tradition, ensuring that the ancient art of tortilla making continues to nourish both body and soul. Their commitment to preserving this culinary heritage is an inspiration, a testament to the enduring power of culture and the importance of honoring one's roots.

The Great Hip Heist

Agnes clutched her hip like it was a winning lottery ticket she was desperately trying to hide. "It's just a twinge," she'd tell anyone who dared ask, her voice a little too high-pitched to be convincing. Her family, however, knew better. They'd witnessed her dramatic, slow-motion descent onto the sofa the other day, a maneuver that involved more groaning than a zombie in a B-movie.

"Agnes," her daughter, Carol,

pleaded, "just go to the doctor. You've been limping for a week."

"Nonsense," Agnes huffed, adjusting her grip on her hip. "It's just a bit… sensitive. Probably just needs a good rub with some… liniment." She eyed the tube of muscle rub on the table, its label boasting the power of chili peppers. Carol shuddered.

"Mom, you tried that last time you 'tweaked' your back. You ended up with a rash that looked like a map of the Amazon rainforest."

Agnes waved a dismissive hand.

"That was different. This is… hip-related."
The real reason Agnes was avoiding the doctor was simple: she hated doctors. Not because they were bad people, but because they asked questions. Questions about diet, exercise, and the last time she'd had a physical. Questions that Agnes preferred to answer with a polite cough and a quick change of subject.
But the pain was getting worse. She was now walking

with a distinct lean, like a ship listing to

port. Getting in and out of her favorite armchair had become an Olympic sport, complete with dramatic gasps and theatrical sighs.

Then, a commercial came on TV. It featured a smiling radiologist explaining the wonders of digital X-rays. "See what's going on inside!" the radiologist chirped. "No more guesswork!"

Agnes's eyes lit up. "That's it!" she exclaimed. "I need an X-ray!"

Carol stared at her. "Mom, you need a doctor to order an X-ray."
"Nonsense!" Agnes declared. "I'll

just... go get one. They have those walk-in X-ray places, right? Like those photo booths at the mall, but for bones!" Carol tried to explain the intricacies of medical referrals and licensing, but Agnes was already halfway to the phone. She found a clinic that advertised "affordable X-rays" and booked an appointment. Never mind that she had no idea what they would be looking for, or how she would explain her self-diagnosis of "hip-related sensitivities."

At the clinic, Agnes charmed the receptionist with tales of her “active lifestyle” (mostly involving brisk walks to the fridge) and her “minor discomfort.” She conveniently forgot to mention the week-long limp and the dramatic armchair incidents.

The technician, a young man named Dave, looked slightly bewildered as Agnes explained she just wanted "a peek at my hip, see if anything's… loose." Dave, used to dealing with actual medical professionals, just shrugged and took the X-ray. Agnes, meanwhile, felt like she'd pulled off the heist of the century. She'd avoided the dreaded doctor's appointment and was now in possession of a picture of her hip.

A week later, Agnes was back at the clinic, clutching the X-ray like a prized possession. "See?" she said to Carol, pointing at the image. "Nothing's broken! Just a bit... shifted, maybe."

Carol squinted at the image, which looked to her like a

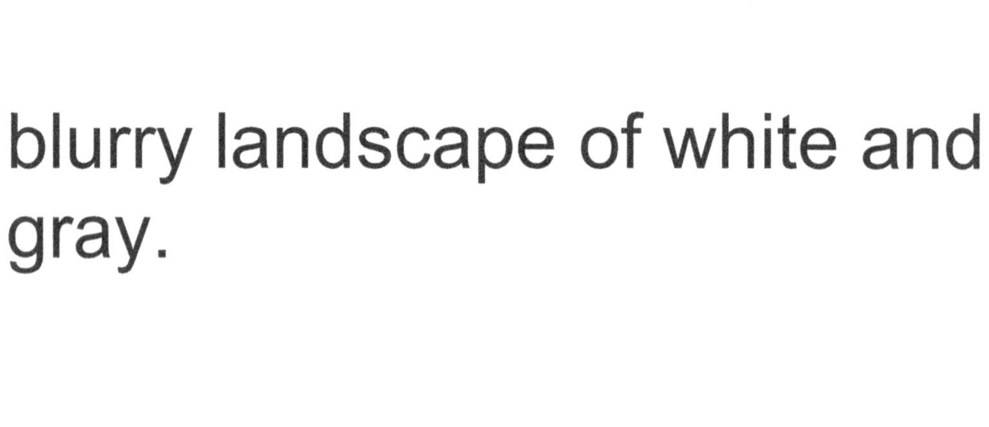

blurry landscape of white and gray.

"Mom, I have no idea what I'm looking at. You still need to see a doctor."

Agnes sighed. She knew Carol was right. But armed with her X-ray, she felt a little more in control. Maybe, just maybe, she could show the doctor the picture and avoid all those pesky questions. After all, she'd already paid for the evidence. Now, all she needed was someone to interpret it… and maybe prescribe something for the pain. And hopefully, that prescription wouldn't involve

chili pepper liniment.

Sangam Bound

In the heart of Bihar, nestled amidst the bustling towns and serene villages, five friends – Rohan, Sameer, Vicky, Riya, and Priya – found themselves yearning for an escape from the ordinary. The call of the Sangam, the confluence of the holy rivers Ganga, Yamuna, and Saraswati at Prayagraj, beckoned them. But the thought of battling traffic jams and shelling out hefty amounts for air tickets dampened their spirits.

One evening, as they gathered by the banks of the Ganga, an idea sparked in Rohan's mind. "Why not hire a boat and journey along the river?" he exclaimed, his eyes gleaming with excitement. The others were initially taken aback, but the allure of a unique adventure soon won them over.

And so, their plan was set in motion. They pooled their resources and hired a sturdy boat from a local fisherman. With provisions packed and hearts full of anticipation, they set sail on a crisp winter morning. The Ganga,

in its majestic flow, guided them through the heart of India.

The journey was not without its challenges. They faced turbulent currents, navigated through narrow channels, and endured the scorching sun. But their camaraderie and unwavering spirit kept them going. They took turns steering the boat, sharing stories, and singing songs to keep their spirits high.

As they drifted along, they witnessed the changing landscapes of rural India. They passed by quaint villages where

time seemed to stand still, lush green fields that stretched as far as the eye could see, and ancient temples that whispered tales of bygone eras. They interacted with locals, learning about their lives, their traditions, and their deep connection with the river.

The evenings were magical. As the sun dipped below the horizon, casting a golden hue on the water, they would anchor the boat and prepare their meals. Under the starlit sky, they would share laughter, dreams, and secrets, their bond growing

stronger with each passing day.

After days of traversing the mighty Ganga, they finally reached Prayagraj. The sight of the Sangam, where the three rivers merged, was breathtaking. They took a holy dip, their hearts filled with reverence and gratitude. The journey had not only taken them to a sacred place but had also deepened their friendship and broadened their understanding of their country's rich heritage.

As they returned to their lives in Bihar, they carried with them memories that would last a lifetime. They had not only avoided the traffic jams and costly air tickets but had also embarked on an adventure that had enriched their lives in ways they could never have imagined.

Finding Faith on the Road

The rumble of the Royal Enfield filled the crisp morning air as Rohan and Priya, a young couple from Maharashtra, embarked on their pilgrimage. Prayagraj, the sacred Sangam, beckoned them, not by the well-trodden paths of trains or planes, but by the open road and the promise of adventure. They yearned for a deeper connection with their faith, a journey that would be as much about self-discovery as it was about reaching their

destination.
Their journey began amidst the bustling streets of their hometown, but soon, the urban sprawl gave way to the serene landscapes of rural India. The bike became their chariot, carrying them through rolling hills, across meandering rivers, and past fields of
gold. Maharashtra's vibrant hues slowly faded into the more muted tones of Madhya Pradesh, each state offering a unique tapestry of sights and sounds.

The first few days were a test of

endurance. The relentless sun beat down upon them, the miles stretched endlessly, and the occasional downpour threatened to dampen their spirits. But Rohan's steady hand on the throttle and Priya's unwavering optimism kept them going. They shared stories, sang songs, and found solace in each other's company. Each evening, they would find a small guesthouse or a roadside dhaba, where they would rest and refuel, sharing chai with locals and listening to their stories.

As they ventured further north, the landscape began to change. The flat plains of Madhya Pradesh gave way to the more rugged terrain of Uttar Pradesh. They crossed paths with pilgrims walking towards Prayagraj, their faces etched with devotion, their footsteps guided by faith. These encounters served as a constant reminder of the spiritual significance of their journey.

One evening, as they were setting up camp by a riverbank, they met an old sadhu. He shared stories of the Sangam, its

mystical powers, and the importance of a pure heart. His words resonated deeply with Rohan and Priya, reinforcing their belief in the sacredness of their pilgrimage. The challenges of the road continued. They faced flat tires, navigated through treacherous potholes, and endured the constant honking of traffic. But through it all, their bond grew stronger. They learned to rely on each other, to anticipate each other's needs, and to face every obstacle as a team.

Finally, after days of riding, they saw it – the shimmering expanse of the Sangam. The confluence of the Ganga, Yamuna, and the mythical Saraswati was a sight to behold. The sheer magnitude of the gathering, the vibrant colors, and the palpable sense of devotion was overwhelming. They took a holy dip in the Sangam, their hearts filled with gratitude and peace. The long and arduous journey had been worth every mile. They had not just reached their destination; they had also discovered a

deeper connection with themselves, with each other, and with their faith.

As they began their journey back to Maharashtra, they carried with them not just the memories of the Sangam, but also the invaluable lessons learned on the road. They had proven to themselves that the journey is often more important than the destination, and that with faith, perseverance, and love, any obstacle can be overcome. The rumble of the Royal Enfield now carried a new resonance, a testament to their incredible pilgrimage.

Where Hope Takes the Bus

The 5:30 AM alarm screamed, a jarring intrusion into the tail end of sleep. Anita groaned, her hand instinctively reaching out to silence the insistent buzz. But the ache in her lower back, a constant companion these days, reminded her that sleep was a luxury she couldn't afford. Forty kilometers. That was the distance separating her from her students, forty kilometers of bumpy roads and erratic bus schedules, forty kilometers that

took a toll on her body, but also fueled her soul.

Anita was a teacher, a calling she'd embraced with a passion that burned brighter than the morning sun. She taught at a small government school nestled in a cluster of villages, a region often overlooked by progress and plagued by poverty. The children, bright-eyed and eager to learn, were the reason she endured the grueling commute. They were her inspiration, her hope for a better future.

The bus, when it finally arrived, was a rickety metal contraption that rattled and groaned with every twist and turn. Anita found a window seat, the cool morning air a brief respite from the ache in her back. She closed her eyes, trying to ignore the jolting motion and the cacophony of sounds – the blaring horns, the chatter of fellow passengers, the incessant squeak of the bus's aging frame. She thought of her students, their eager faces, their inquisitive questions. That

thought was her anchor, her motivation.
The journey was a trial. The roads were uneven, riddled with potholes that sent shivers through her spine. The bus driver, a man seemingly impervious to the discomfort of his passengers, navigated the treacherous route with a reckless abandon that left Anita's stomach
churning. Each bump was a fresh stab of pain in her lower back, a reminder of the physical toll her dedication was taking.

By the time she reached the school, the sun was high in the sky, casting long shadows across the dusty playground. The children, dressed in their simple uniforms, rushed towards her, their faces alight with smiles. Their enthusiasm was infectious, a balm to her weary body and spirit.

The day was a whirlwind of lessons, laughter, and the occasional scolding. Anita taught with a passion that belied her physical discomfort. She poured her heart and soul into

every lesson, determined to give these children the education they deserved. She saw potential in each of them, a spark that she nurtured with unwavering dedication.

The backache, however, was a constant presence. It throbbed during her lessons, a dull ache that intensified with every step she took. Standing for hours, writing on the blackboard, bending over to help a student – each movement was a struggle. But Anita persevered, driven by her commitment to her students.

The return journey was even more challenging. The bus was packed with weary travelers, the air thick with the smell of sweat and dust. Anita's back screamed in protest, each jolt sending a wave of pain through her body. She leaned against the window, her eyes closed, trying to find a position that offered some relief.

Back home, the silence was a welcome change. Anita collapsed onto her bed, the exhaustion finally catching up with her. She thought of the next day, the same grueling

commute, the same throbbing pain. But she also thought of her students, their bright eyes, their thirst for knowledge. And she knew, despite the struggle, despite the pain, she would do it all again. Because for Anita, teaching wasn't just a job, it was a calling, a commitment, a love that transcended the physical challenges. It was a journey she was willing to endure, one aching kilometer at a time.

Closing Chapter

The Tapestry of Moments

The old wooden chest, overflowing with its jumble of memories, finally felt a little lighter. Each story I'd pulled from its depths, each experience I'd relived and written down, had taken a piece of the past and woven it into the present. This book, born from a simple desire to capture the everyday magic, had become more than just a collection of anecdotes. It had become a tapestry of moments, a vibrant record of a life lived,

loved, and learned.
Closing the chest, I ran my hand over its smooth, worn surface. It wasn't just a container for the past; it was a symbol of the journey itself. The scratches and dents, the faded varnish, each told a silent story of its own, mirroring the imperfections and triumphs that had shaped my life.
I looked around my small writing room, the room where so many of these stories had come to life. Sunlight streamed through the window, illuminating dust motes

dancing in the air. It was a quiet,

ordinary moment, yet it felt imbued with a special significance. Perhaps because now, after months of delving into the past, I was acutely aware of the preciousness of the present.

This project had taught me that the extraordinary often hides within the ordinary. It's in the shared laughter over a simple meal, the quiet comfort of a familiar routine, the unexpected kindness of a stranger. It's in the way the sunlight catches the leaves of a tree, the scent of rain on dry earth, the feeling of a

warm hand in yours. These seemingly insignificant moments, when strung together, create the rich and complex fabric of our lives.

I realize now that the stories I’ve shared aren't just my own. They are echoes of the universal human experience. They speak of love and loss, joy and sorrow, fear and courage. They remind us that we are all connected, bound by the shared thread of our humanity.

As I close this book, I don't feel a sense of finality, but rather a sense of continuation. Life, after all, is a story that is constantly being written. New chapters are added every day, filled with new experiences, new challenges, and new moments of grace. And just as I have woven the threads of my past into this book, I will continue to weave the threads of my present and future into the ever-evolving tapestry of my life.

This book is not an ending, but a beginning. It's an invitation to look closer at the world around you, to appreciate the beauty in the mundane, and to cherish the

fleeting moments that make up a life. For within those moments, you will find the magic, the wonder, and the story of you. And that, I believe, is the greatest story of all.

Acknowledgments

I am deeply grateful to the many people who have contributed to the creation of this book.

First and foremost, I want to thank my parents, for their unwavering love and support. Their sacrifices and encouragement have shaped me into the person I am today.

To my beloved wife, thank you for your constant love, patience, and belief in me. Your unwavering support has been my strength throughout this journey.

My children, have been a constant source of inspiration. Their laughter, love, and curiosity have enriched my life in countless ways.
I would also like to express my sincere gratitude to my extended family and friends, who have always been there to offer encouragement and advice.
Lastly, I thank the countless individuals who have touched my life and contributed to my growth. Your support has been invaluable.

Other books by Aditya Mani Gupta

1.Echoes of the Bygone Era

2.My Reflections

Available on draft2digital.com partners and Kindle

amazon kindle

05 DEC 2024

PUBLISHED

BARNES & NOBLE

05 DEC 2024

Rakuten kobo

06 DEC 2024

Get it on Apple Books

05 DEC 2024

Everand

06 DEC 2024

tolino

05 DEC 2024

OverDrive

11 DEC 2024

08 DEC 2024

BAKER & TAYLOR

06 DEC 2024

hoopla

Long Processing Times

18 DEC 2024

ODILO

05 DEC 2024

vivlio

05 DEC 2024

BorrowBox.

05 DEC 2024

05 DEC 2024

11 DEC 2024

Gardners

05 DEC 2024

fable

06 DEC 2024